GIRLS' HEALTH ™

SEXUAL ABUSE

MARYLEE FLORIC AND MATTHEW BROYLES

rosen publishing's
rosen central®

NEW YORK

Published in 2012 by The Rosen Publishing Group, Inc.
29 East 21st Street, New York, NY 10010

Library of Congress Cataloging-in-Publication Data

Floric, Marylee.
Sexual abuse/Marylee Floric, Matthew Broyles.
    p. cm. — (Girls' health)
Includes bibliographical references and index.
ISBN 978-1-4488-4572-9 (library binding)
1. Child sexual abuse—Juvenile literature. I. Broyles, Matthew. II. Title.
HV6570.F58 2012
362.76–dc22

                                        2011006186

Manufactured in the United States of America

CPSIA Compliance Information: Batch #S11YA: For further information, contact Rosen Publishing, New York, New York, at 1-800-237-9932.

CONTENTS

INTRODUCTION

Everyone wants to be loved. Like most people, you want your parents to cherish you and your teachers to recognize your work. You want your friends to like you. Affection and love can be expressed in many different ways. Sometimes you may get hugs and kisses; other times you may get a pat on the back. These gestures are important and make you feel good inside. Being noticed can make you feel more confident and accepted. These are healthy feelings, and they remind you that you are special in a way that nobody else is.

Maybe someone you admire is giving you extra attention, or an older friend or relative is hanging out with you more often. This feels great because someone who is older and more experienced recognizes how cool, smart, and mature you are. He or she recognizes the talents that you have and makes you feel important.

This attention can sometimes become confusing, however. When a pat on your back becomes a pat on your backside, you may feel uneasy. You may question or doubt yourself, wondering why you feel strange or why you've attracted attention that doesn't feel good anymore. It's hard to admit that someone you trust makes you feel uncomfortable. But remember: if someone is making you feel strange or uncomfortable, you are not imagining things. Your discomfort is valid, and you should distance yourself from that person and his or her behavior, even at the risk of jeopardizing what seems like a really cool and developing friendship.

If you are uncomfortable around someone, don't be afraid to speak up. No one should touch your body without your permission. If they do,

When someone's attention makes you feel uneasy, you might be asking yourself, "Did I somehow send out a wrong signal?" Your unease is reasonable, and you should distance yourself from that person.

they are not showing you the respect that you deserve. When someone touches or treats you in a sexual way that makes you feel uncomfortable, it's called sexual abuse. Sexual abuse is not an expression of love; it is hurtful and destructive. Tell someone who is in a position to help about the abuse. Seek help from a trusted adult, either in your family, school, or community. Keep speaking up until you get the help you need to stop the abuse.

CHAPTER one

THE MEANING OF SEXUAL ABUSE

"**S**exual" means activities associated with parts of your body that can give you great pleasure when you are very aroused, attracted to someone, and/or in love. The main sexual organs that give the body pleasure are a girl's vagina and clitoris and a boy's penis. These body organs are used in reproduction and are called genitals. Touching other parts of the body such as the breasts, backside, leg, or mouth can also be sexual.

"Sexual abuse" means using someone else's body for sexual pleasure without his or her consent, and this is a crime. Sexual abuse usually involves the abuser's contact with the sexual organs of the victim's body. The abuser may touch a young person's sexual parts or ask the person to touch his or her sexual organs. Or the abuser may use the young person in some other sexual activity. For example, a male may force his penis into a girl's vagina (when the penis enters the vagina, it is known as intercourse; when it is a forced act—against the other person's will—it is rape). A female abuser may force a young boy to have intercourse. She can also force a young girl to give or receive genital stimulation. A man may abuse a boy by demanding to give or receive oral or anal sex or touching of the penis. When a child has sexual contact with a parent, brother, sister, or other close blood relation (including half-siblings, aunts or uncles, grandparents, and cousins), it is called incest.

The majority of young people who are sexually abused are abused by someone they know and trust.

FACTS AND FIGURES ON SEXUAL ABUSE

If you are being sexually abused or have been abused, you are by no means alone. As reported by the American Psychological Association (APA) in 2010, 35.9 percent of the victims of sexual abuse are children ages twelve and older. According to research by the Centers for Disease Control and Prevention (CDC), one in four girls are sexually abused before the age of eighteen. Almost 60 percent of sexual abusers are known to the child but are not family members (such as family friends, babysitters, or neighbors).

Accurate figures on the widespread presence of sexual abuse of young people are difficult to collect because it is greatly underreported. Never be ashamed to tell someone if you are being abused.

Nearly 30 percent of sexual abusers are family members (such as fathers, brothers, uncles, or cousins). It is estimated that there are as many as sixty million survivors of childhood sexual abuse in the United States today.

Despite the prevalence of sexual abuse in the home and sexual assaults by relatives or acquaintances, it is estimated that less than half of all sexual assaults are reported to the police. This is probably due to the fact that victims of sexual assault—especially victims of sexual abuse by a family member or relative—are filled with fear and a sense of shame. Their abusers often encourage these reactions to dissuade them from telling anyone about what happened. The victims may feel deeply embarrassed, guilty, and dirty, despite the fact that the abuse is not their fault. Only the abuser should feel guilt and shame.

Many victims of sexual abuse are too afraid, embarrassed, or conflicted to report the crime. If you're being abused, don't be embarrassed to tell someone. Sexual abuse is never your fault. You didn't ask for it or invite it. It is the abuser's fault and his or her shame, not yours. The abuser needs to be stopped and prevented from abusing someone else. Furthermore, he or she needs to get professional help. The only way this will happen is if you speak up to a responsible adult who will get you the assistance you need.

CHAPTER two

EXAMINING SEXUAL ABUSE

Sexual abuse is not always clearly understood by people, even by those who have been victims of it. The following information should help clear up many misconceptions about sexual abuse, its victims, and its perpetrators.

SEXUAL ABUSERS–WHO ARE THEY?

When you were young, you were warned about strangers who try to grab or hurt young people. Those persons are called child molesters. Child molesters are often, but not always, male. And they are usually thought of as strangers. It's important to realize, however, that child molesters can be women, and they can be people known to you, such as a teacher, neighbor, family friend, or family member. According to the APA, women are the abusers in about 14 percent of cases reported among boys and 6 percent of cases reported among girls.

Did you know that children and teens are much more likely to be sexually abused by a person they know well, such as a teacher, scout leader, neighbor, doctor, coach, minister, family friend, or the father of a friend? Many teens are even abused by members of their own family, such as a brother, father, stepfather, uncle, grandfather, or older cousin. The family members who most often sexually

A high school English teacher and basketball coach is being led to a courtroom for sentencing after his trial. The man was found guilty of attempted rape and other crimes, including sexual abuse involving a seventeen-year-old female student.

abuse children are fathers and brothers. Sometimes, however, even mothers abuse their children.

The hardest thing about sexual abuse is that the abuser is usually someone you trust. It may be someone who is responsible for taking care

Young people are taught to respect and obey older people. If your abuser is an adult, you must find a way to say no to the abuser. You have to trust another adult to tell him or her about the abuse so that you can get help.

of you. It may be someone you love. The problem is that you may not know how to act or what to say when this trust is betrayed and you are sexually abused by a loved one.

The first step in dealing with sexual abuse is learning how to say no. The problem is that saying no to an adult or someone you trust is not always easy, but it must be done. The next step is to get help. This won't be easy, either, because you will have to once again place your trust in an adult. Having just been abused by a trusted adult, it will be hard to trust another adult to help you stop the abuse and find the assistance you need. For your own physical and emotional health, however, you must do it. The abuse must stop, and the abuser must be removed from your environment. Ideally, he or she should also be prosecuted, jailed, placed in therapy, and prevented from ever abusing anyone else ever again.

ARE THERE SPECIFIC FAMILY CHARACTERISTICS?

A myth is something that is commonly believed to be true by many people but is in fact false. One myth is that sexual abuse only happens in families that have a lot of other problems, too. Some abusers do have serious mental health problems. Some are sexually attracted to children, but not to other adults. And some abusers were sexually or physically abused themselves when they were children. Some families where sexual abuse occurs also have other problems. The husband may be beating his wife, for example. Or one or both parents may be alcoholics or addicted to drugs.

But most sexual abuse occurs in seemingly ordinary families and is committed by seemingly ordinary people. These abusers may have good jobs and nice houses. They may be leading members of the community, perhaps active in their church or local politics or the PTA. There is no quick, visual way to identify a sexual abuser.

What is typical of most sexual abusers, however, is that they want things their own way. Though they may claim to be offering you love and devotion and special attention and consideration, they are in fact selfishly seeking to grab something that does not belong to them, simply to gratify their own desires. They like being in control and having power over others. This is why they are attracted to those who are smaller, weaker, and less sure of themselves than they are, like children and teens.

DO ALL SEXUAL ABUSERS USE PHYSICAL FORCE?

Many sexual abusers use physical force. Others use threats. Others convince their victims to submit to them without complaint by preying on their sense of guilt, fear, desire to be loved, and confused feelings. The abuser may threaten to harm someone the child loves, such as the victim's mother or the family pet. Or a father may say he will leave the family forever if the child tells anyone about what is going on. He may even claim that a policeman will take the child away. As a result, the child may start to fear the very people who can rescue him or her from the abuse.

Sexual abuse doesn't always involve physical force or threats. Many abusers use bribes or presents to convince the child to do what they want. Money, candy, a new video game, new clothes, a shopping spree, or promises of a special trip are held out as lures to buy the child's silence and submission. An abuser who is a relative may try to convince the child that he or she is a favorite, that the two of them are misunderstood by everyone else and need to form a secret bond. This preys on many children's natural desire to belong and to feel cherished, special, and uniquely appreciated.

Often sexual abuse begins as a game, such as tickling or playful wrestling. After the abuser gains the child's trust, the game's touching becomes sexual. By disguising the sexual abuse as a game, the abuser can always claim that the victim misunderstood his or her actions or the touching was accidental and just part of the usual clumsy fumbling of any physical game.

WHAT ARE THE LASTING EFFECTS?

Sexual abuse can cause serious hurt and damage problems, even when there is no violence or intercourse. Children who are abused feel isolated from other children. They may feel ashamed about what has happened. They may think they are not worth much, so they have low self-esteem. They may feel so angry that they hurt another child or a pet. Or they may try to hurt themselves. Some children who are sexually abused become very sad or withdrawn. This is called depression.

Sexual abuse can also cause problems when a child becomes an adult. Adults who were sexually abused often don't trust others. They may want to avoid sex entirely. Some victims will act out sexually, trying to reenact the original trauma over and over again, perhaps in an effort to reach a different outcome or exert some control over a situation that made them feel totally lacking in control.

Perhaps most disturbing, victims of sexual abuse can often go on to become sexual abusers themselves. Forty percent of sexual offenders and 76 percent of serial (repeat) rapists claim they were sexually abused as children, according to Dr. William C. Holmes, a researcher at the University of Pennsylvania School of Medicine. Female victims of sexual abuse who do not receive counseling, treatment, or other kinds of help face similar problems in the future.

The longer sexual abuse goes on, the more damage it can cause. In general, male and female victims of abuse experience increased feelings of fear, guilt, anxiety, depression, anger, low self-esteem, alcohol and drug abuse, lack of trust, difficulty forming close relationships, inappropriate sexual behavior, and even violence, both in childhood and as adults.

Young people who have been abused sometimes have low self-esteem and become bullies. They become very angry and at times take out their rage on someone younger.

Not all children who are sexually abused suffer lasting effects. If the abuse is stopped early, the abuser is removed from the child's environment, and the child finds a trusted person to talk to, many of the longer-term harmful effects of sexual abuse can be prevented. Professional counseling is also enormously helpful in allowing the victim a healthy outlet for all his

Teen volunteers with the Clothesline Project in California hang some T-shirts that are covered with messages to raise awareness about the victims of sexual abuse. Rape, domestic violence, and child molestation survivors wrote the messages.

or her fears, confusion, and anger. It can also help the person realize that he or she is an innocent victim and bears none of the blame or shame for what has happened. The person who sexually abused the victim is sick and needs help. He or she also committed a criminal act and needs to receive the appropriate punishment.

HOW HAVE PEOPLE BECOME INFORMED ABOUT SEXUAL ABUSE?

Everyone learns about sexual abuse when people who have been sexually abused tell their stories. Adults who were hurt by sexual abuse as children are now talking about it. Young people are pushing past their fear and embarrassment and are beginning to talk, too. They are telling their stories to anyone who will listen and is in a position to help and sympathize. Parents, doctors, teachers, police, therapists, and others who want to help and protect young people are learning about sexual abuse and how best to help and protect victims. Young people all over are speaking out, refusing to be silenced, shamed, or intimidated. For this reason, sexual abuse is the secret that is now being shared, and many victims are not continuing to live with the burden of fear, anger, and sorrow placed on them by their attackers.

MYTHS
AND
FACTS

MYTH **Sexual abuse is most often committed by strangers.**

FACT Most sexual abuse is committed by someone the victim knows and trusts.

MYTH **A child or young person who has been sexually abused will grow up to be a sexual abuser.**

FACT Many children who are sexually abused do not become child sexual abusers when they grow up. But many sexual abusers were abused themselves when they were young, and they never received therapy for the trauma. Forty percent of sexual offenders and 76 percent of serial rapists claim they were sexually abused as children.

MYTH **Only females are victims of sexual abuse.**

FACT According to research by the CDC, one out of six boys and one out of four girls are sexually abused before the age of eighteen.

CHAPTER three

THE MOST COMMON FORMS OF SEXUAL ABUSE

Sexual abuse is always devastating. The victims of sexual abuse often feel isolated, confused, and distrustful of others. There are many different types of sexual abuse. Two of the most common are incest and rape.

DEFINING INCEST

Incest is any sexual activity between people who are closely related to each other. Someone who is closely related to you can be a family member, like your father, mother, brother, sister, half-sibling, grandparent, cousin, aunt, or uncle. Traditionally, incest has been defined as sex between two people related by blood. But incest can also occur between members of a family who aren't necessarily blood relations, like a stepfather, stepsister, or uncle by marriage.

Any sexual activity between a child and another family member can be called incest. Incest is not limited to the act of sexual intercourse. If a member of your family touches private parts of your body, that is considered incest and it is a form of sexual abuse. If a family member makes you look at or touch parts of his or her naked

A newspaper headline in Melbourne, Australia, refers to a man who supposedly raped his daughter every day for thirty years and fathered her four children. About 30 percent of perpetrators of sexual abuse are family members.

body, that also is incest. When a family member forces you to look at or pose for pornographic pictures (pictures that involve sexual acts or situations), that is incest, too.

WHO IS GUILTY OF INCEST?

Incest can happen in families that are rich or in families that are underprivileged. It can happen in homes where parents are living together or in homes where parents are divorced, separated, or remarried. Although the abuser is often male, that is not always the case. Sometimes the abuser is a female family member. The type of incest that is most difficult for a child to recover from is that committed by a parent. Children trust their parents to protect them from harm. When a parent sexually abuses a child, that trust is shattered.

Incest occurs most often in homes in which the abuser was a victim of incest as a child. Incestuous abusers may prefer to keep their family to themselves and avoid contact with outsiders. They don't want their behavior, which they know is wrong, to be discovered by others. They may try to keep their victimized family member or members from having friends to prevent them from telling someone about the abuse.

When an abuser is discovered, he or she may not accept responsibility for his or her actions. He or she may make excuses or try to blame someone else. For instance, a father might try to justify his incestuous actions by saying that it is better for him to have sex with his daughter than with a woman outside of the family. He may even claim that his daughter seduced him or that unhappiness with his wife drove him to it. A lonely mother might approach her oldest son for sex if her husband is dead or disabled or has left the family. But the truth is that incest can never be justified. It is always wrong. It is always the abuser who is to blame. Abusers usually know that what they are doing is wrong.

INCEST'S VICTIMS

Incest is a particularly destructive form of sexual abuse. It destroys family members' trust in one another. Victims of incest are often justifiably angry and feel betrayed by their abuser because they once trusted that person with their lives. Incest victims may also be angry with other members of the family for failing to protect them, recognize what was going on, or do anything about it.

Sometimes family members fail to recognize the warning signs of sexual abuse within the family. Sometimes they refuse to acknowledge the abuse even when they are told about it. It can be very hard, even for adults, to believe that someone in their family could commit such a horrible act. It is also hard to struggle with the guilt of not recognizing the abuse and intervening to halt or prevent it. Sometimes it feels easier to live in denial than have to face these harsh family truths.

If this is the case in your family, if you can't get anyone to listen or believe what you're saying, go outside the family to find someone who will listen and act to protect you. If you think you may be the victim of incest, tell someone—a school counselor, a teacher, a friend's parent—what is going on. Keep talking until someone takes action to stop the abuse and get you into a safe environment.

RAPE AND RAPISTS

Rape is the crime of forcing a person to have a sexual encounter against his or her will. This means the forced act of putting a penis in someone's mouth, anus, or vagina. Rape, like all acts of sexual abuse, is most frequently committed by someone the victim knows. The rapist may be a

A teen cringes in fear after being assaulted by her boyfriend. Among victims ages eighteen to twenty-nine, about two-thirds had a previous relationship with the perpetrator of sexual violence.

member of the victim's family, a family friend, or a community leader such as a teacher, coach, or spiritual leader. Both men and women commit rape. Rapists are most often adults. However, other children or young adults can also be guilty of rape. The victims are often children and teens; 18 percent of rape victims are under age twelve, and 44 percent are under age eighteen.

Many rapists were sexually abused themselves. People who are sexually attracted to and rape children are known as pedophiles. Pedophiles are usually heterosexual (meaning they have sexual feelings toward people of the opposite sex). When pedophiles have sex with someone their own age, they often prefer women. When they rape a child, however, they do not always choose a victim of the opposite sex. Sometimes, they choose a victim of the same sex.

THE CONSEQUENCES OF RAPE

Like all forms of sexual abuse, rape can cause long-lasting emotional problems for the victim. Rape victims often battle for years with shame, guilt, depression, and anxiety. Rape can also cause physical injury and enduring health problems. Delicate body tissues can be torn or damaged during rape. Rape victims often bleed or are literally scarred as a result of being raped.

Another health concern for a rape victim is sexually transmitted diseases (STDs). A rapist who has an STD can pass this disease on to the victim. AIDS is the most dangerous STD; there is no cure for it. Other STDs such as gonorrhea and syphilis can cause permanent damage if they are not treated quickly. They can even be life-threatening if they are left untreated. Pregnancy can also result from rape if the victim is a girl or a woman of childbearing age.

Because of all the possible health complications that can result from rape, it is extremely important for a victim to seek medical attention immediately. A victim of rape should go directly to an emergency room without

A medical professional opens a rape kit at a lab. Rape victims should seek medical attention at once. At the hospital emergency room, a doctor or nurse will take samples that can be used as evidence against the accused rapist.

showering, changing clothes, or cleaning up. The doctor or nurse will take samples of bodily fluids and hair, which can be used as evidence if you decide to report the crime to the police. If you do choose to press charges, vital evidence needs to be collected within the first twenty-four hours after the assault. If you miss this time frame, it is still possible to gain evidence. And for your own health, you should still see a doctor. It is also important to save any clothes you were wearing at the time of the assault and don't wash them. Put them in a plastic bag and store them somewhere safe until you decide what is best for you.

Each year, thousands of cases of sexual abuse, including rape and incest, go unreported. Many children worry that if they report incest, they will be taken from their homes. Others fear that the abuser will be sent away, perhaps to prison. But sexual abuse is a crime. What happens to a sexual abuser is never your fault. Sexual abusers must be forced to stop their pattern of abuse or they will continue to abuse you. They may also be abusing other people. When you report a case of sexual abuse, you help protect yourself and other potential victims. There are programs designed to help sexual abusers stop their destructive crimes. Remember, even if the abuser is your mother or father, keep talking until someone listens and helps you.

CHAPTER four

ONLINE PREDATORS

Computers are everywhere, from cash registers to cell phones and other mobile devices to cars to airplanes. If you use a computer regularly, you've probably been on the Internet, too. The Internet can be a great place to learn new things or talk to people about common interests.

CHAT ROOMS

The Internet has places that people can visit on their computers to discuss their interests with others. These are called chat rooms. Chat rooms can seem like a great way to make new friends. However, they can be dangerous, too. You should use caution when having conversations on your computer with strangers. In a chat room, all you know about this stranger is whatever he or she chooses to tell you. And what he or she tells you may not be true. Chatting on a computer gives you a false sense of security and anonymity. It makes you feel like you can say anything or let someone else say anything.

Yet you should think of a chat room as a physical space and the person you're chatting with as a person standing there with you. This person is a stranger, and you wouldn't immediately start talking to a stranger in an intimate way. This person may be nice

An officer with the Peachtree City Police Department in Georgia logs into a chat room to help crack down on sexual predators who prowl the Internet. Nearly one in five American youths who surf the Internet are targets of unwanted sexual attention.

and friendly and entirely innocent. However, he or she may also intend to deceive and harm you. You just can't know, and you don't even have the usual physical cues of a face-to-face encounter to help give you an impression of that person's personality and intentions.

Some sexual abusers are using the Internet to find victims. They use a chat room to make friends with a young person, often by pretending to be a child or teen themselves. They convince their victim to meet with them personally and then sexually abuse him or her. Some teens have even been murdered after being molested by predators they met on the Internet and agreed to meet with. Some cyber predators also encourage teens to e-mail naked or otherwise sexually suggestive pictures of themselves or film themselves in suggestive poses using a webcam. These images can then be used for the predator's personal gratification, or he or she may distribute them widely across the Web.

SOCIAL NETWORKING SITES

Web sites such as Facebook and MySpace—social networking sites that allow people to post personal profiles, blogs, videos, and photos—have caused increasing concern among parents, school administrators, and law enforcement officials because of the opportunities they offer for online predators.

The Federal Bureau of Investigation (FBI) has several suggestions for preventing sexual abuse for kids and teens who use the Internet:

- Never give out identifying information such as your name, address, phone number, or photograph to anyone without first getting your parent's permission.

- Never respond to messages that are obscene, suggestive, threatening, or that make you feel uncomfortable in any way.

- Always tell your parents (or a trusted adult) if someone makes you feel uncomfortable.

- Never arrange a face-to-face meeting with anyone you meet on the Internet unless you have your parents join you and you meet in a public place.

If you do begin to receive e-mails or chat room solicitations that make you uncomfortable or are sexual in nature, tell your parents immediately

Mark Zuckerberg, chief executive of Facebook, explains the social networking site's latest privacy control measures. Many Americans are concerned about exposing themselves and their kids to companies that gather personal information via cell phone and the Internet for marketing purposes.

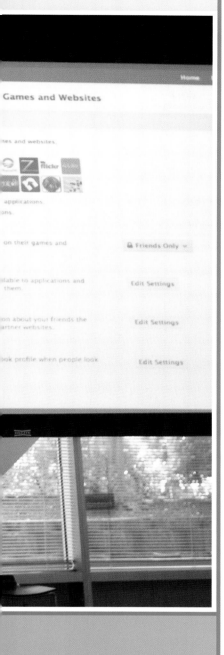

and contact your local police. Just because the inappropriate behavior is occurring online and not in person, it is still objectionable and illegal sexual contact and activity. The abuser is getting sexual gratification from being in contact with a minor, and he or she may also be hoping that it will lead to a face-to-face meeting in which physical abuse can take place. Don't let this happen to you or anyone else the predator may be contacting. Alert the authorities to this person and help make both the cyber world and the real world a safer place.

CHAPTER five

RECOVERING FROM SEXUAL ABUSE

Sexual abuse hurts victims physically and emotionally. A number of programs are specially designed to help victims cope. If you have been sexually abused or if you are currently being abused, it will be extremely helpful if you find and participate in one of these programs.

COUNSELING

Even if you are no longer being abused, you may feel anger, hostility, and shame, and you may feel as if you have little control over your own body. Someone has used your body without your permission and that makes you feel violated and defenseless. You may experience periods of anxiety or depression. It will take time for you to heal. But you will heal.

The negative emotional effects of sexual abuse can continue into adulthood if you don't seek help. The love and support of caring family members and friends can help ease your mind during the rough times to come. You may wish to speak to a professional therapist, perhaps one who specializes in treating forms of sexual abuse. You may also want to find other survivors of sexual abuse with whom you can share your feelings.

Victims of sexual abuse must cope with a number of confusing emotions. It is best to talk with someone, such as a professional therapist or counselor, who understands the emotions that abuse victims feel.

FINDING A THERAPIST

A therapist is a professional who is trained to listen and help people sort through their emotions. It is possible to find a therapist who works primarily with victims of sexual abuse. A therapist can be an employee of a mental health agency or a family and child protective services agency, or he or she can operate a private counseling practice. You can ask your school counselor or another adult to help you locate a therapist.

You can also find a therapist on your own. If you have reported your sexual abuse to a human services agency (such as family and child protective services), you can call your caseworker at that same agency. He or she should have a list of experienced sexual abuse therapists in your area. Even if you have not reported your case, a human services agency is a good place to begin your search. Your medical doctor may also be able to put you in contact with a sexual abuse therapist.

The next step is to make an appointment to see one of the therapists. The therapist is there to help you. A good therapist will not attempt to force you to talk about anything that makes you uncomfortable. For the most part, he or she will do a lot of listening. Therapists will support and reassure you and help improve your emotional well-being. Therapists do not judge you; they know what you've been through, and they sympathize completely. They know how to help you through the trauma of sexual abuse, and they want to help you through it.

You may feel comfortable right away talking to the therapist. However, if you do not feel comfortable right away, don't be alarmed. This is a new experience, and it may take a few appointments for you to feel at ease. It may be that the therapist is simply not the right one for you. As with any other person you meet, you may hit it off or you may not. Make an appointment to speak with another therapist if you consistently feel inhibited from speaking freely. Chances are you will feel more comfortable talking with another therapist. It's absolutely OK to switch therapists. Therapists are very interested in creating the best possible matches between clients and counselors.

INDIVIDUAL COUNSELING

Individual counseling gives you the chance to share your feelings about sexual abuse and its effects on you in a private atmosphere. Only you and the therapist are present. He or she knows that you are not to blame for the abuse. There is no need for you to feel any pressure to discuss aspects of the abuse that you are not ready to talk about yet. The therapist knows from experience with other victims that talking about abuse can be difficult and painful. Some victims may feel uncomfortable talking about the abuse for weeks, months, or even years. If you are not ready to talk about the abuse or your feelings concerning it, your therapist may use other methods to try and help you, or he or she may ask you what you would like to discuss.

Some victims of sexual abuse prefer to write about their feelings in a journal and then allow their therapist to read the journal. Others may want to draw a picture or make a painting to express themselves. Children in particular often use dolls or puppets to show their therapist what type of abuse they suffered. A therapist should allow you to express yourself in whatever way you find the most comfortable.

The amount of time needed for counseling is unique to each person. Someone who was abused once is likely to need less counseling than someone who suffered repeated abuse over a long period. Nevertheless, a single instance of sexual abuse is traumatic, and you should not feel pressured to get over it quickly or get down on yourself if it continues to haunt and hurt you. Just concentrate on confronting and working through your feelings and accept that there is no time limit on that process.

GROUP COUNSELING

Many sexual abuse victims feel isolated from their peers. They have suffered abuse that makes them feel different from their friends. A victim may feel as though he or she is the only person who has suffered in this way. Victims who have these feelings may benefit from group counseling. Group counseling consists of a small number of victims and a counselor who leads the group's discussions. Many groups are made up of members

When they are ready, some victims choose group therapy, which will offer support to them and other members of their family. Therapists can help victims associate with others and develop the ability to trust and have relationships again in a group setting.

of approximately the same age who have shared similar upsetting or traumatic experiences.

Group counseling gives a victim the opportunity to meet and talk with others who have experienced similar abuse. Group members realize that they are not alone, and they learn from each other. They learn how to cope with and express their feelings in a healthy way. They learn how to deal with family members and friends. Group members learn that they can depend on support as each of them faces new emotional challenges relating to the abuse. By learning to depend on one another, victims begin to trust other people again, which is an important step in the healing process.

Most sexual abuse victims undergo some individual counseling before they feel ready to join a group. Many therapists feel it is helpful for victims to continue with individual counseling and participate in group counseling. It is up to you and the therapist to decide what type of counseling or combination of counseling is best for you. Ultimately, it is your choice to create the kind of therapy course that you wish to follow and is the most helpful for you.

OTHER COUNSELING OPTIONS

Many sexual abuse victims feel anger toward their parents. Abuse victims may feel let down by the failure of one or both of their parents to protect them. If this is the case for you, you may benefit from counseling with one or both of your parents. It may prove helpful to discuss these feelings under the guidance of a therapist. A good therapist will help you direct your anger in other directions so that it will not harm you or anyone else. He or she will also gently encourage you to raise the issues you have with your parents and talk through them, making sure both sides are hearing and understanding what the other is saying. If your family is to function in a healthy manner, it is essential that your faith in your parent or parents be restored.

Perhaps you have been sexually abused by one of your parents. You may wish to participate in ongoing counseling with your abusive parent. But such counseling sessions should never be forced on you. You should have the right to decide when you feel ready to confront your abusive parent or if you wish to confront him or her at all. You may decide to wait a few months or even years. Or you may decide never to confront him or her with the abuse. This is a highly personal and individual decision. Just try to listen to your best instincts and consult with your therapist. Any decision you make now can always be revisited later.

A T-shirt that reads "You killed my soul . . . but not my spirit" pays tribute to a young victim of sexual abuse. Recovery and healing from sexual abuse is a process that takes time, and that time varies from person to person.

When your parent abused you, he or she wrongly assumed control of your body. Now you have the opportunity to be in control instead of your parent. You can decide when and if you talk together in therapy, and with the help of your therapist, you can set the agenda.

The world can seem like a scary place in which you have very little control over events and people's behavior. If somebody is abusing you or someone you know, remember the rules and tell someone immediately. You can cope, recover, heal, and live a healthy, happy life. Take the first step—speak up.

10 GREAT
QUESTIONS

1 If someone in my family touches me in ways that he or she doesn't touch any of the other kids, should I tell someone?

2 Someone touched me in a way that I wasn't comfortable with and told me not to tell or I would get in trouble. Should I tell?

3 Sometimes my dad and my brother or sister go into a room together for a long time, and they won't talk about what happened while they were in there. Should I tell someone?

4 I told my mom about how I don't like the way one of our family members touches me, and she said to keep it to myself. Should I tell somebody outside our family?

5 I've been talking to a kid on the Internet who wants to meet somewhere without my parents around. Should I go?

6 I think I was raped, but everybody tells me that boys can't be raped. Is that true?

7 A woman touched me in a way I didn't like, but no one ever talks about women being abusers. Can women be abusers?

8 If I tell what happened to me, what will happen to the person I'm telling on? What steps should I take if I want to file a police report?

9 I know that being sexually abused is never the victim's fault, but what I can do to help make sure it doesn't happen again?

10 I am feeling a lot of different emotions after my experience. Is that normal?

GLOSSARY

abuser Someone who hurts you sexually.

affection The physical expression of a gentle feeling of fondness or liking.

agenda A list of items to be considered and discussed at a meeting.

depression Sadness; a state of unhappiness and hopelessness; a type of mental disorder showing symptoms such as persistent feelings of hopelessness, dejection, poor concentration, lack of energy, inability to sleep, and sometimes suicidal tendencies.

devotion Love, loyalty, or enthusiasm for a person, activity, or cause.

dissuade To persuade someone not to take a particular course of action.

genitals Sexual organs.

heterosexual Having sexual feelings toward people of the opposite sex.

incest Sexual activity between two people who are closely related.

inhibit To make someone self-conscious and unable to act in a relaxed way.

intercourse When a male's penis is placed inside the vagina of a female.

jeopardize To put someone into a situation in which there is a danger of loss, harm, or failure.

misconception A mistaken idea or view resulting in a misunderstanding of something.

molester Someone who forces sexual contact on someone else.

obscene Indecent or offensive.

pedophile An adult who enjoys sexual activity with children.

perpetrator Someone who carries out something morally wrong or criminal.

pornography Pictures, films, or stories that clearly show sexual activity for the purpose of arousing sexual desire.

prevalence Being widespread; the number of events being present at a given point in time.

prosecute To take legal action against someone.

rape When one person forces another person to have sexual relations.

solicitation A request for someone to do something; a request to get someone to participate in immoral acts.

STD (sexually transmitted disease) A disease, such as AIDS, gonorrhea, or syphilis, that can be passed from person to person through sexual contact.

stimulation Causing someone to become interested or excited about something; causing a body part to respond to something.

submission The action of accepting or yielding to the will or authority of another person.

survivor Someone who was hurt or abused in the past.

therapist A person trained to help treat mental or physical problems.

traumatic Extremely frightening, distressing, or shocking, and sometimes having long-term mental effects.

victim Someone who is being hurt or abused.

FOR MORE INFORMATION

Assaulted Women's Helpline (AWHL)
P.O. Box 369 Station B
Toronto, ON M5T 2W2
Canada
(866) 863-0511
Web site: http://www.awhl.org
This helpline is available twenty-four hours a day, seven days a
    week, for all women who have experienced abuse.

Canadian Society for the Investigation of Child Abuse (CSICA)
P.O. Box 42066
Calgary, AB T2J 7A6
Canada
(403) 289-8385
Web site: http://www.csicainfo.com
The CSICA was formed in 1985 in response to a growing need for a
    coordinated, professional approach to child abuse investigations.

Childhelp USA
15757 North 78th Street, Suite #B
Scottsdale, AZ 85260
(480) 922-8212
Hotline: (800) 4-A-CHILD (2-2-4453)
Web site: http://www.childhelp.org
This national nonprofit organization provides hotlines and focuses on
    research, prevention, and treatment of child abuse.

Child Welfare Information Gateway
Children's Bureau/Administration for Children and Families

U.S. Department of Health and Human Services
1250 Maryland Avenue SW, 8th Floor
Washington, DC 20024
(800) 394-3366
Web site: http://www.childwelfare.gov
Child Welfare Information Gateway promotes the safety, perma-
nency, and well-being of children, teens, and families by
connecting child welfare, adoption, related professionals, and
concerned citizens to timely, essential information.

Darkness to Light
7 Radcliffe Street, Suite 200
Charleston, SC 29403
(866) FOR-LIGHT (367-5444)
Web site: http://www.darkness2light.org
Darkness to Light is a national nonprofit organization devoted to
reducing child sexual abuse nationally through education and
public awareness aimed at adults.

National Alliance to End Sexual Violence
1101 Vermont Avenue NW, Suite 400
Washington, DC 20005
Web site: http://www.naesv.org
This national organization works on public policy and advocacy for
victims of sexual assault.

National Center for Victims of Crime
2000 M Street NW, Suite 480
Washington, DC 20036

43

(202) 467-8700

Web site: http://www.ncvc.org

This national organization deals with advocacy, education, and
    helping victims of crimes.

Rape, Abuse and Incest National Network (RAINN)

2000 L Street NW, Suite 406

Washington, DC 20036

(800) 656-HOPE (656-4673)

Web site: http://www.rainn.org

This is the nation's largest antisexual assault organization. It operates
    a hotline and does advocacy work.

WEB SITES

Due to the changing nature of Internet links, Rosen Publishing has
developed an online list of Web sites related to the subject of this
book. This site is updated regularly. Please use this link to access
the list:

http://www.rosenlinks.com/gh/sex

Carter, William Lee. *It Happened to Me: A Teen's Guide to Overcoming Sexual Abuse*. Oakland, CA: New Harbinger Publications, 2002.

Crosson-Tower, Cynthia. *Sexual Abuse of Children and Adolescents*. Boston, MA: Allyn & Bacon, 2005.

Ferro, Jeffrey. *Sexual Misconduct and the Clergy* (Library in a Book). New York, NY: Facts On File, 2005.

Feuereisen, Patti, and Caroline Pinks. *Invisible Girls: The Truth About Sexual Abuse*. Emeryville, CA: Seal Press, 2005.

Gerdes, Louise. *Sexual Violence* (Opposing Viewpoints). Detroit, MI: Greenhaven Press, 2008.

Gorden, Sherri Mabry. *Beyond Bruises: The Truth About Teens and Abuse* (Issues in Focus Today). Berkeley Heights, NJ: Enslow Publishers, 2009.

Haley, John, Wendy Stein, and Heath Dingwell. *The Truth About Abuse*. 2nd ed. New York, NY: Facts On File, 2010.

Hoffmann, Kerry Cohen. *Easy*. New York, NY: Simon & Schuster, 2006.

Lanagan, Margo. *Tender Morsels*. New York, NY: Knopf, 2008.

Lehman, Carolyn. *Strong at the Heart: How It Feels to Heal from Sexual Abuse*. New York, NY: Farrar, Straus & Giroux, 2005.

Lundgren, Mary Beth. *Love, Sarah*. New York, NY: Henry Holt & Co., 2001.

Mather, Cynthia L., and Kristina E. Debye. *How Long Does It Hurt? A Guide to Recovering from Incest and Sexual Abuse for Teenagers, Their Friends, and Their Families*. San Francisco, CA: Jossey-Bass, 2004.

Rainfield, Cheryl. *Scars*. Lodi, NJ: Westside Books, 2010.

Rosen, Marvin. *Dealing with the Effects of Rape and Incest*. New York, NY: Chelsea House, 2002.

INDEX

A

AIDS, 24
alcohol abuse, 13, 15
American Psychological Association (APA), 7, 10
anal sex, 6, 23
anger, 15, 18, 22, 32, 37
anxiety, 15, 24, 32

B

betrayal, 13, 22
blogs, 29
breasts, 6
bribes, 14

C

Centers for Disease Control and Prevention (CDC), 7, 19
chat rooms, 27–28, 29
child molesters, 10, 28
clitoris, 6
counseling, 9, 13, 15, 17–18, 19, 22, 32–38
crime, 6, 18, 23, 25, 26

D

denial, 22
depression, 15, 24, 32
doctors, 10, 18, 25, 34
disability, 22
divorce, 21
drug abuse, 13, 15

E

e-mails, 29

F

Facebook, 29
family and child protective services agencies, 33, 34
family therapy, 37–38
Federal Bureau of Investigation (FBI), 29
female abusers, 6, 10, 12, 21, 22, 24, 39

G

genitals, 6
gonorrhea, 24
group counseling, 35–37
guilt, 9, 14, 15, 21, 22, 24

H

heterosexual, 24
Holmes, Dr. William C., 15
human services agencies, 34

I

incest, 6, 20–22, 26
individual counseling, 34–35, 37
instincts, listening to your, 37
intercourse, 6, 15, 20
Internet, 27–31, 39

J

jail, 13
journals, 35

M

mental health agencies, 33

ABOUT THE AUTHORS

Marylee Floric is a writer who lives in Minneapolis, Minnesota.

Matthew Broyles has written several books for young adults. He now resides near Dallas, Texas.

PHOTO CREDITS

Cover, p. 1 © www.istockphoto.com/Aldo Murillo; pp. 5, 7, 8 istockphoto/Thinkstock; pp. 11, 28 © AP Images; p. 12 © www.istockphoto.com/Richard Clark; p. 16 © www.istockphoto.com/Christopher O Driscoll; pp. 17, 38 © The Orange County Register/ZUMApress.com; p. 21 WILLIAM WEST/AFP/Getty Images; p. 23 © Jim Varney/Photo Researchers, Inc.; p. 25 © LA Daily News/ZUMApress.com; pp. 30–31 Kim White/Getty Images; p. 33 © www.istockphoto.com/Chris Schmidt; p. 36 Zigy Kaluzny/Stone/Getty Images.

Designer: Nicole Russo; Photo Researcher: Amy Feinberg